A review of my career in school administration…

…in the field of education with the Rochester City School District….

Welcome to the…

The Principle Role of the Principal

-for teachers, administrators and others to enjoy!

Alexander C. Johnson

November 18th, 2012

Rochester, New York

TABLE OF CONTENTS

CHAPTER 1
The Move from the Classroom to "Helping Teacher"

CHAPTER 2
Searching for other "Avenues" to Assist Teachers, Students and Parents

CHAPTER 3
The Challenges and Goals of the Principalship…
…with Strong Principles

CHAPTER 4
Children, Parents and Staff in Binding Them Together for Educational Success

CHAPTER 5
My Own Background in the My Educational Career

CHAPTER 6
Creating the New Role of the Substitute Principal in the Rochester City School District

CHAPTER 7
A Look Ahead in Education…as a Retired Principal…
…for Principles Ahead

CHAPTER 8
Some Thoughts to Consider in Doing the World's Most Important Work... Teaching Children and Others to Aspire to a Greater Life

CHAPTER 9
A Reflection on Good Administration
Alex J. Johnson, National Board Certified Teacher, 2011

CHAPTER 10
Personal Thanks to my Family, the R.C.S.D., Local Colleges, and the Thousands of Parents and Students

CHAPTER 11
A Chronological Timeline on How I Reached My Professional Goals

CHAPTER 12
Final Thoughts for Those That Aspire to the Field of Education as Either Teachers or Administrators

APPENDIX 1: My Educational Timeline   pp. 76 - 77

APPENDIX 2: Schools Where I Served   pp. 78

APPENDIX 3: Documents   pp. 79 - 87

APPENDIX 4: Photographs   pp. 88 - 97

Preface

In this book, **The Principle Role of the Principal**, I review my career in education by recollecting what led me into my life's work in associating with children, parents and school administration. In this examination, I look for the clues, ideas and motivation that led me in education from the classroom, which I enjoyed, to the "chair" of the principal. Therefore, this book is my career from the alpha to the omega, the beginning to the end of my working in education. I hope this will give guidance of what one educator has done, and perhaps for others to follow, to have a successful career.

In addition to my initial career with the Rochester City School District, I spent another 10 years as the first "substitute principal" in the RCSD. After 43 years in education, I decided to re-retire in the year 2000 and attend to other matters pertaining to family, organizations, and volunteer activities.

I feel that this journey in the educational world will show a concerned teacher who always felt that the school was the foundation of our society, and therefore needed to be looked at carefully. This look into my career will demonstrate my concerns, hopes and dreams for a strong American educational system for the success of our society. I wish to share this message with family members (many of whom are in the field of education) and others who aspire to enter the field of education. It is a most worthwhile career that builds a solid society in America and throughout the free world.

I would like to dedicate this book to my family, mainly my wife Ginny, who always encouraged my changes in the field of education, and supported me in the happy and challenging days.

Enjoy reading this book for the betterment of education, and for the structure of a great America, in relationship with the world today and tomorrow.

ACJ

The following are some of the ideals and goals that I have lived by and were taught to me by my parents years ago...

...God bless them!

"Look to the future and seek new goals rather than think about lost events from the past"

"They will always look for the educated one...."

"Study hard and win a star for life in accomplishments"

"Everyday is a day to learn and love knowledge that can last forever"

"Find a Good Teacher and you have found a GOLD MIND"

"The future lies in finding new knowledge to learn and act upon"

"The only thing standing between ME and greatness is ME... a thought to keep in mind as we strive toward individual and collective achievements"

CHAPTER 1

The Move from the Classroom to "Helping Teacher"

It all started when I, a teacher happily working with children, got the desire to spend more time with all the students in my school. Should I move to the position of a school principal in order to reach a greater number of children and thus provide them with the positive goals of learning and eventually a better life? Should I aim to reach out into the community to work with the P.T.A. and school administration for the sake of the many children beyond my classroom? These were a couple of the questions I asked myself as I considered going beyond the classroom to sit in the principal's chair.

I am now looking back to 1962 when I was a very satisfied teacher with the City School District in Rochester, New York. I'd had success as a teacher in the 4th, 6th and 7th grades and really loved the classroom. My first move towards administration was in that year when I moved from the classroom for a brief try as a "helping teacher". This was a position that had me working with newly hired teachers, as I was only five years earlier. Would this role lead me to an administrative position or maybe a return to my 'first love' of working in my own classroom? Only time would tell, but there I was, helping the ten teachers assigned to me and to assist them in becoming better teachers for the sake of our great responsibility which was to the children that we were charged with and to make a better future life for each.

In speaking to my supervisor, Mrs. Lillian Brooks, who entrusted me with this great responsibility of helping these teachers, I accepted this challenge and made my tour of the various schools around the city to set good goals for our new teachers. Day by day, I reached beyond my own classroom to these various teachers so they could develop skills to work successfully with our children in our district.

All this challenge gave me a great satisfaction to serve as a "role model" for others to follow and enlarge our skills to reach out to many more beyond one school. This good feeling began to grow within me, as these can be the principles of our goal to become a good principal.

As the year moved on, I travel to all of my assigned ten schools to meet up with the first year probationary teachers who were under my charge to review their progress in working with children and setting goals for their success to a tenured teacher in time. The challenge was not to change their personality or manner of operation since all of my ten teachers were different from each other but to gain their confidence in establishing a rapport of building their skills and reaching more success.

Some of my teachers showed a great deal of success already and indicated a promise to establish new achievements in their daily work. Those I highly encouraged to keep building forward on to new heights and accomplishments in their work with children. Often I felt a kind compliment was in order to encourage the teacher to move on and not get discouraged if "things went wrong that day or week" but to build on past success and focus on the next step. Most did and that pleased me indeed as I felt like I was doing my job correctly and that gave me more motivation to do it again and again with the other teachers.

Of course there were some teachers who had many difficulties in establishing good rapport with children or parents and needed much guidance in order to show an improvement in their work.

Again, I tried to guide and build within them an introspective review of their talent to reach out to children in a positive manner and correct any disciplinary problems that were obvious in the classroom. That often times worked and success was gained after a few weeks of focus in that fashion. Unfortunately, there were a couple that were "not making it" and I had to point that out to the individual teacher and move them toward the thought of leaving the profession and seek another career with which they could find success their future.

I was so pleased to hear from two of those teachers months later in that they were thankful that I counseled them to move on to another career. One was a young man who just was not able to build a strong discipline system with his students. He realized that "something was missing" in his work and therefore he did not have it in his heart the desire to stay since he missed the success mark that he was after. He called me months later on to tell me that he went into sales work and was very happy in his new career and thanked me for helping him "find the way" into a new career. Another was a more experienced teacher who for years was not able to move children along in achieving higher grades. I saw the removal of several children from her room in order to make it easier for her to reach success with those remaining....but it was not working. Again, I had to counsel her to consider retirement since she was of that age and could leave at the end of the school year. Well, she retired and months later, I had a visitor come to my office. Mrs. B. was now a picture of happiness as she was dressed very well and looked peaceful and calm. With a big smile on her face, she said, "Mr. J. that suggestion was the best thing you could have done for me...I am very happy now doing volunteer work and just love my new role in life." Indeed, she was very happy and reached a time of her life that moved her into success in another role. We were both very pleased.

These two events and others that followed happened because of positive counseling and that made my work successful in helping our school district reach the goal... "reach out to every child " and help our teachers gain success with our children each day and each year. Often times, teachers are so close to the "problem" of their work that they do that they do not recognize the entire situation. Therefore, it takes a non-threatening person, like my role as "helping teacher", to point out the needs and possible solutions. Some of these solutions are obviously achievable and in some cases….fortunately… only a few….were not reached.

The role of reaching out to teachers who are moving toward tenure (a permanent contract) is a very important since they are building up practical experience and valuable teaching strategies and skills. Training from college courses and perhaps some sub work now becomes reality in the making. The reality is the day to day skill building and reaching children with many needs….personal, social, environmental and of course their academic ability.

Even after "tenure appointment at the end of 3 successful years of teaching", the continued need that I always tried to enact into the teacher's future career was to constantly build their skills toward perfection….for the sake of the child this year and for the rest of the teacher's career. Tenure, as I explained to the teachers, was an appointment to move forward in becoming a master teacher with knowledge, ability, new skills, patience and love for the profession.

As the three years unfolded in working with probationary teachers, I wanted to establish a rapport with each staff member. I worked with each teacher to win over their trust and confidence so that the "post-grad involvement" as a first, second and third year teacher, the real world of education opened up to them. This opening was to meet parents who were the first teachers of our children and the child's siblings in order to better understand family circumstances and seek avenues of communication to reach each child better. Often, what we see of a child in the classroom is only the surface of the child and there is a need to get into the depth of the mind of each to better reach the child in achieving success. Each child is an individual with strong ties to his/her parents and may reflect these traits in the school. A better understanding of the home environment is so important to understand the child in his social and developmental progress in the classroom.

The RCSD always seeks the best way to establish a solid base of teachers who can build each child's skills to the fullest. One of the ways the district does this is to have good supervision of teachers in guiding them and establishing "role models" for them to follow. In the year that I became a "helping teacher" working in several schools, I felt a strong compulsion to build confidence in the new teachers and give them guidance for success. I honestly feel we did that and that it was so very important in having a successful school system...i.e. establishing a strong foundation for each and then stand behind them each and every day in the most crucial work....building solid citizens for tomorrow.

The role was so important to me since I felt that it gave me a deep insight into the working of the school system and gave my teachers a deeper understanding of what was crucial for our children. It was, and always should be ..."for the children", since they are the basis for our being a team in building the rapport with parents in the understanding of our educational system.

I would like to add that my experience as a "helping teacher" and later as a supervisor of teachers, aided me greatly in giving myself a solid foundation for the administrative work that I took on as a vice principal, and later as a principal, of several schools in the district for over 33 years. The foundation also helped me greatly as a parent, along with my wife, to guide our five sons throughout their education in their formative years and on to undergraduate and graduate school as well.

CHAPTER 2

Searching for other "Avenues" to Assist Teachers, Students and Parents

As I completed my year as a "helping teacher" and had a feeling of accomplishment, I knew that there could be other "Avenues" to travel to help teachers, students and parents with whom I may be working with in the future of my career in education. The RCSD did offer interested educators a chance to take an exam and present qualifications for school administration as a vice principal and principal of our schools. I did take the exam and went through the "in-basket/out-basket" routine of dealing with situations and having interviews to help set a foundation for going into administration. My interest was now very much "peaked" as I looked beyond the present year of my career.

Upon completing my exams and interviews, I was granted the approval to go on to the next step in my career in education. I was given my first assignment as a vice principal (supervising teacher) at two different schools for the following school year. I was to spend two and half days at each school working under the direction of two different principals at the schools assigned. I thought this would be an interesting challenge since each principal was quite different from the other (both being very good in their own way) and I would have to make allowances in dealing with each with their own personalities and special focuses. Indeed, it was a challenge but a most worthwhile experience as the doors opened for me in the next year. I accepted the challenge and felt it would be a good learning experience for me and that new knowledge would help me reach out to the teachers and children that I was charged with at those schools. I almost felt like a conductor leading a big orchestra with many members….the instrumentation would be important indeed…in order to stay on the same page but to have each member reach our goals in an individual way for the benefit of all.

In my first assignment as a vice principal, I was assigned to work at a K-6 school in the inner city of the RCSD. My other school was to be in a similar sized school but with children with more diverse background. Every child in each of these schools was a precious challenge to the teachers as we worked to direct their learning in the proper direction. I always felt that we had to look at each child as an individual with a particular need. This need with the support of the parents and the foundation building of the school would help each child reach their goal successfully.

As I worked in each school, I had many varied responsibilities in each building. I was involved in making certain that the proper scope and sequence was followed by each teacher and the curriculum was covered at each particular grade level. This was very important since with a wide variety of talented teachers who had their strengths, and sometimes a lower level of understanding in certain subject areas, that the children were never "short-changed". I accomplished this by checking "plan books" and made certain the pacing and coverage was made with instruction each week. Also the need to make certain that the proper materials were made available from our "book room" to the new students who arrived at our school from other buildings within the RCSD and from afar. Sometimes the curriculum was quite different from their former schools and some briefing had to be done in order to get the child "up to speed" in our our classrooms and school.

I found that working in two different schools presented a strong challenge in that I needed to have good knowledge of the 35 some different teachers' abilities and their developmental progress in the profession. It was a real challenge but it kept me on my toes to be alert and learn with them as we made progress. I felt that it did benefit me as I was aware of larger pool of talents, strengths and abilities that I could share with various teachers in a similar way that I did the year I was a "helping teacher". This exposure gave me additional knowledge to share with various teachers who needed this additional background to make them stronger teachers over time.

As the year went on, additional needs had to be met by me in working with the teachers. There was a requirement to "evaluate" each teacher assigned to me with a formal evaluation by a particular deadline. I gave the teacher a guideline sheet so they could describe the lesson in some detail so that I could follow the steps taken in the instruction for that lesson. It was a relatively simple guide but most important since it gave me a good overview of a "map of direction" with the objective(s), materials used, special information about the lesson or a child and anticipated goal of the lesson. After notifying the teacher of a specific time, I would come into their classroom to observe them. As I observed the teacher, I was able to note the ability of the teacher to meet these goals by taking notes down for myself. These notes I later shared with the teacher at our post observation discussion of the lesson. Often times, the lesson did meet the objectives very well and we discussed that at our conference. Sometimes, I had to note that the lesson was not really getting at the real objective of the plan and therefore some follow-up was needed to be done. Obviously, it was always a good thing to point out the positive things of the lesson and give praise to the teacher for their achievement. In most cases, there always were strong points in the lesson that needed to be discussed and that would build a stronger foundation for the teacher to build on for other developmental lessons which were going on each day. At some point of the evaluation conference, any needs or corrections had to be discussed and a strong look to improvement was made at this time. Usually, there was good acceptance on the part of the teacher to make any changes as may be necessary. I always tried to leave the teacher with a strong feeling of good accomplishment in a lesson very well done or an observation that with some correction of the lesson could become more successful. I always tried to see the positive flow of the lesson and build on that to gain higher levels of achievement for the students and the teacher for the future. Each lesson was like a fine artistic painting that needed to be completed with the "right color, correct strokes…shades and shadows". This would bring the masterpiece to a total completion, with a minimal of correction or over-lay of work to bring out the full "beauty of the lesson".

I was fortunate to be at the beginning of the "computer-age" with this new technology in the RCSD. I was one of the first principals (with only 3 – 4 other schools participating in this new pilot program) to have access and complete teacher evaluations on this wonderful modern medium for record keeping. This was a real advance from record keeping in a written form and sent via courier to our personnel office for review. Now, each principal or vice principal, could record the outcome of lessons on the spread sheet, print a copy for the teacher and the office file and then send it on to Central Office. It certainly was a fast and efficient way for updating files and records. We had arrived at the computer age of record keeping and transmission in that first year of my computer involvement.

At the tenure review, all the files could be brought up on the computer and a reviewed a with clear knowledge of the past. A scan of past reviews were easily made and progress noted from lessons observed.

In addition to the observation by the principal or vice principal, we also had departmental personnel come to observe a teacher in order to get a more "in depth" review of the lesson, especially in the "specials" areas as Music, Physical Education or Art. This review gave the administrator more information about some of the special needs of the lesson and also gave another view of a specialist in order to reach a successful lesson's goal. I always welcomed other specialists to our school in order to have a more solid understanding of our "map to success" as the year moved on for the sake of the children and the teacher.

CHAPTER 3

The Challenges and Goals of the Principalship…

…with Strong Principles

Who really is the principal with principles in reaching the strong goals for the child, teacher, school and district? How are these principles developed so that success can be reached? These are a couple of questions I had in mind when I first got the idea of writing about my 43 plus years in the profession of education in the American public schools and my several years teaching during my military service in Indiana and South Korea.

My feeling now, that I have worked many years in the field, is that the person must be leader, role model, administrator, guidance counselor, disciplinarian, record keeper, good public relations person, friendly with a happy smile (even though sometimes it is difficult to do that), a temporary mom and dad and a person who is ready to take on any action that is necessary to accomplish the job successfully. The principles develop in time with on the job training as it were, but…some innate talent and desire to do this work should be present as one goes into the field. These principles must always be for the sake of the child to bring success to his/her life and to build a stronger tomorrow for the child, teacher, parents and yes, even the country, all starting in the classrooms all over this nation.

As the principal works with so many people from staff and children to parents, community leaders and Central Office personnel, these principles are formulated to always, I repeat always, with the aim of the betterment of the student, the school and school system. I have always believed that we are in the school business for the children's sake and not be in it just for the money. The children always come first.

At this point, as one of my principles of working with parents, I would like to say a few things about the need to get to the foundation of knowing the families. As often it is said, the parents are the child's "first teachers" and with a successful laying of the foundation of life, the child will be ready to come to school for his/her formal training in the skills needed for life. I always felt that as principal (and as a teacher too), it was very important for us to be as close to the families as possible. In this closeness, we can observe reactions, attitudes, feeling and the circumstances of the family. While we learn about the families, we can also leave diplomatic hints of what can be done in order to better the families' patterns of child rearing. Sometimes little has to said but at times, carefully pointed suggestions can make a real difference. These differences can improve child/parent relationship or help build a good attitude toward the child for better learning or improved attendance. Each point of positive reaction can help bind us with the families for a partnership as we need to travel this road together. This "road" of travel can bring success for the child for years to come. I have seen this happen many times…working with parents who needed a lot of good advice or some who seemed to be resistant but welcomed a few kind hints. We can all use help in life, especially when it comes to our children, the future of our community or our country.

One aspect of this needed parent partnership is to help the parents to come to school as often as possible. I always announced to teachers and parents, that my door was always open and that I would welcome them to speak with me and exchange ideas. Sometimes these talks would lead to more participation of the parent to "see" what we are doing for their child so the parent could then continue this action at the home for better outcomes for the child. Parents, I feel, are for the most part, very interested in their child and want the best for each of them. If the parent and school personnel see "eye to eye" and work as a team, success can be achieved more often than not. So, the principle stress of the principal needs to be "togetherness" as a team working with the families to be there for the child. Often times other relatives in the family can assist in building a solid foundation for the child also. Sometime a relative (grandmother, grandfather, uncle, aunt, etc.) may have skills and can be used as role models for helping the child reach new heights in achievements. It sometimes takes more than a family to raise a child....at times more than a "village"...but we all have to take a solid stake in wanting and be willing to guide, assist and model for the child for them to move up in the world. Again, it takes teamwork to get the job done.

Transparency is a much used word today in politics and it should be part of the school view of having all options on the table for the "team" to understand where we have been and where are going in planning a solid instructional program for the child. In this school transparency, there is a strong need to have an "open door policy" as I have had for years in my work at various schools. (See Cathleen Corbet's letter on page. 88 who welcomed this manner of operation). This open door policy is not only for teachers but very important for parents so that the invitation is always out to welcome them in and talk. Any concerns the parents have can be discussed and a possible solution found in the discourse. I have always felt that parents were a vital part of the solution and most want to be just that. Sometime a parent may be reluctant to come in a talk over a problem. However if they realize that the door is "open" to them in this endeavor for transparency, they want to and will come in to be part of the solution. I loved to see parents come in and give me their input in order to help the school and most important, their child succeed.

Through use of the PTA / PTO and school bulletin (or newsletter) principals can easily inform the parents of their open door policy and willingness to communicate freely about their concerns with the administration.

Children are the "root" of our existence in a school system and they also need to be part of the team that I have been mentioning. I often times had children come in to review their progress in their classroom and show paper work or projects that they had completed. This built pride in their achievement and gave them more incentive to move further ahead and upwards. Between the teacher, principal and parent, the child hears success in their work and gives them more desire to even do better as their self-esteem builds. That is a very normal feeling most humans have…encouragement and a positive attitude developed will give one the desire to move onward. I did this with my teachers when I was a "helping teacher", vice principal and certainly now with children as this principle became part of my engagement as principal. Again, this encouragement needs to be shared with the "home team". That beautiful beaming smile of a student is a wonderful reward to see as one presents praise for the fine accomplishment.

Even today, many years after my retirement, I so enjoy seeing a young man or woman come up to me and say, "Aren't you Mr. Johnson who was my principal at school #----" "Yes, indeed, I am", I reply. Many of these former students will say, "I really appreciated what you told us or did for us" or they'll remember things that I may have forgotten over the years, but to the then child, it meant the world to them and it adhered in their mind for all those years. I like to think that the success of these young people (perhaps thousands that I have been in contact with over the span of my career) happened with those precious moments that the teacher, or parent with the teacher, or any person in the school implanted the seeds of success. It all starts in the home, the foundation and our schools build, repair, renovate or promote the future positive outcomes for the child turning into the adult of tomorrow.

I believe the truth in education lies in building principles of life as early as possible in order to accomplish a positive outcome for the adult of tomorrow. This is one reason why my career was dedicated in being in the elementary schools, in order to help build that strong foundation for life. The secondary schools do a very important job of building solid skills and in-depth understanding of subject matter that will prepare the future doctor, lawyer, nurse, chef, business person, teacher, etc. However, all these stages of life in building careers need a solid starting point. This starting point, I feel that we at the elementary schools, must provide that solid level of foundation for the future. The principles of a strong work ethic and desire to move forward in academic achievement always start with the family and dedicated school personnel who unite as a "team of educators" for the child.

It is exceedingly important for school personnel (teachers, specialist, supervisors, principals) to reach out to parents as early as possible to "build a team" of motivating individuals that will reach out to their child and keep the pace moving throughout all the years of their education. I have seen the success of this in my working with hundreds of parents and teachers. I now see the same in my retirement years with our five sons, four daughter-in-laws and our twelve grandchildren who are now in elementary school, high school, college and beyond. Each year, from the early years to college years and even graduate work, there is a continued need to motivate, encourage, reflect and help in any way possible to keep the child "on the road to success". This is needed in order to complete the goal set before all of us as parents, educators and related personnel who need to be part of the team.

We need ALL of you…to be part of the team to build success…onward we travel on the road of educating our future. Everyone is important since it takes a team to get the job done successful!.

CHAPTER 4

Children, Parents and Staff in Binding Them Together

for Educational Success

Here I would like to look at the beginning "nuts and bolts" of the major point of this chapter….starting the "hub" of children, parents, staff in binding them together for success.

As I looked back in my career of being a teacher, supervisor and principal, I think back to how the hub of a team gets started. Many times, words are easy to say but difficult to do if there is no set plan of action. This plan of action must start out at faculty meetings, PTA meetings, conferences with parents and even at PPS meetings (Pupil Personnel Services) where teachers, principals, social workers, school nurses, psychologists meet. Each of these units is most important to set goals, set standards, evaluation points and anticipated outcomes.

A common goal must be established early in the engagement of the group or staff. This goal must center on the child of course as we make plans of action for teaching and learning in the days and years to come. I often tried to build a rapport within the group of personnel so that we would work as a team for one cause...the success of our children as we move ahead.

Record keeping is important in order to stay on course of "where we have been and where we are going". At each meeting of the team, we would try to project our goals so that we are all working together for the sake of the child. Bringing in the parents onboard is very important in order to formulate a true team spirit of action. At times, I have noted in my records of the child, that missing information from the cumulative record file could be explained by the parent. Perhaps that information was not noted for a special reason or it was never asked for at registration and it is most significant for the sake of enlightenment of the staff of potential problems in learning. I have found that a good rapport with the parents was very important in order to find out about possible problems for the student's social / academic work and to learn how we can correct these issues. This open door policy was the key to my working with parents and staff. Open communications with the home is most important in order to reach success for the student.

I always felt that there were other key personnel in the school that had a large role to play in helping students, the school staff and the community. These key persons are the school secretaries (administrative assistants) and custodial engineers that help keep the school running. The first person most parents and staff meet when they enter the school office is the school secretary. This person can well set the tone for the arrival and make him/her feel at ease and positive. Often when I had to leave the building for a while, I felt like I had to turn over the reins of the school to my secretary to "run the school" until my return. This was before the death of Peter Castle and we were required then to have a "teacher-in-charge" ... before the establishment substitute principals. A talented secretary can work the computers, keep office records and make visitors feel welcomed and important. I have been blessed with many wonderful secretaries through my 43 years with the RCSD. Their talents displayed to the public is so important to the positive outcome of many problems which we deal with daily. Many of them should be given a "star" for their achievements and my thanks to them was a token of appreciation to their efforts and all that they did. In looking back now, I really think I was lucky to be surrounded by these wonderful people who often "made my day".

The other group of staff who help "run the school" are the custodial engineers who not only bring us heat, a comfortable atmosphere and cleanliness but assist in solving a whole array of problems. Sometimes a school's problems are not possible to solve without their help. I well recollect some of these wonderful men and women who would help direct parents to the office, assist with children who need a caring person to lean on or keep the school secure for everyone's safety. I have one person in my mind that was truly just wonderful to go well beyond his duties all the time to help everyone. They are the guardians of the school who "make it happen" when the need is there. Thank you from again to all of you who made our school warm, cool, clean, safe, friendly and a workable atmosphere. Thank you, thank you very much to the "extra" non-teaching personnel who we could not do without.

There are many other people that help make our children and school successful. These "protectors" and supporters in our area are the firefighters, police and civic leaders, who all had a positive interest in making our goals successful. So often I had to call on the local police to help locate a lost child or to escort a child to safety when parents could not be found. Or, when firefighters came many times to visit our school to teach fire safety and observe many fire drills so that we could evacuate the school within 2 minutes in any kind of weather…just in case! The local civic leaders who came to PTA sessions and "Open Houses" to observe and comment on the many achievements that we have been making throughout the year, all this helps motivate us to "do more" for the success of our children each day, each week and each year.

Again, it takes a total team effort to make "the school stay on target" and find solution after solution in classroom achievements, social, educational, safety and other elements of human involvement. I always felt that it took a "team" to develop the child from home to school and back home…if we want to be successful in our work.

I trust the reader can now formulate in your mind that the "hub or center that I mentioned at the beginning of this chapter is coming into focus as we look at the CHILD and then process all the team members of direct or indirect contact with our children…all taking a part in the action of reaching positive outcomes to the completion of our goals. The steps through the pre-school, elementary, secondary levels and on to a good employment in life or a college education and then a professional position that he/she, the parents, the school and of course society has a part of the action in total.

A short story about how negatives can be turned into a positive outcome may be mentioned at this point…involving one of my children and his parent at one of my many schools that I served as principal.

I was sitting at my desk in the my office when all of the sudden, a woman appeared at my door with "fire in her eyes". She took off her wig and threw it at me, almost hitting me in the face. She charged in toward me and said, "If I had a gun, I would shoot you"…." "You had no right calling my son such a 'bad name' as he came home to tell me what you said." She continued. I need to explain what happened prior o this exchange. Her child left school without any permission to tell his mother this false story. The child was sent down to my office for misbehavior and told he was not allowed by the teacher to go on the class field trip. He was to wait in the office until the class returned. I saw the boy and told him, "You must wait here and do your assignment while your class is on the field trip since you were misbehaving in class this morning". The child grunted something to me and was not very happy about the matter. I told him to stay there and do his work and I would talk to him shortly because I was doing some important paperwork for the school at the moment. In a short time, I went out into the outer office to speak to him and noticed that he was gone! I checked the hallways and around the school and could not find him. I came back to my desk trying to call home to see if he went home. This is when the mother came dashing into my office. At this point, I tried to calm her down by talking softly and trying to get the story clear in our minds. I continued to tell her what happened regarding the field trip, how he was supposed to do his work but rather left without permission and went home and made up a false story of my calling him a real bad name. We talked and before too long, the mother saw that her son's story was made up. She then started to tell me about her personal life and how some man had done her harm years ago and upset her and on and on.... I tried to be a good listener and spoke softly and acknowledged her misfortunes in life. I gave her some good solid counsel about human behavior when she got off her chair and approached me and planted a kiss on my check and said, "You are a good man Mr. Johnson, you understand me". I thanked her for coming in and she took her son home with a positive feeling about the school. This was "one for the books", I felt at that moment and said to myself, "If I ever write a book about my school career, I will have to include this true story"…now, I just did!

I am writing this information here to record the need for patience and understanding among the people that you associate with in daily life. This is especially true in working with all kinds of parents / guardians in a school system, the cooperative and not so cooperative type that one encounters in a school family. I often encountered irate parents who fail to have an understanding of all strong efforts to build a solid foundation for our children and the school in general. This is probably one of the most important principles of being a good school principal....and of course a good teacher as well. Build, build and build until you see the strong foundation for success.

I trust the reader will see the great value in this endeavor to build a strong home connection.

CHAPTER 5

My Own Background in the My Educational Career

At this point, I would like to take the reader to the start of my "thinking about being a school principal" and seeking those principles of dreaming, wishing and acting toward the goal in order to move forward in my career.

As with the start of everything goal oriented, you need to have a far look into the future set goals of where you want to be in the years ahead. I had my dream for many years of going into teaching and then perhaps becoming a school principal. I wanted to work with people in improving their lives…especially children's lives.

I would like to recall for you the steps I took educationally after graduating from Niagara Falls High School in the Class of 1950. I achieved my first degree in education from the State University of New York at Brockport (B.S. Elementary Ed.), I worked my way through college (with some family financial assistance) at the Eastman Kodak Company, Sibley's Department Store, The Taylor Instrument Co. and other employers in order to move ahead with my principles of life. I kept my goals in mind and tried to set a definite plan of action in place.

After graduation, I joined the U.S. Army and while in the military I taught at an elementary school in Indianapolis part time when I was stationed at Fort Benjamin Harrison in Indiana. I was later stationed in Seoul, in post-war South Korea in the 1950's. I was asked if I would be interested in driving my jeep to an engineering school about four miles away from our base and meet with a group of South Korean Army officers who wanted to learn English. Some of them spoke just a little English but out of the twelve, I believe half did not speak any English at all. So the goal was to establish a fundamental alphabet and a guide book to learn the beginning sounds and sentence structure of English. That was a little challenge but it was done. The students were very appreciative and worked hard to learn and did so quickly. Since they were knowledgeable and studious men, their growth was very obvious from one week to the next. We met for two days a week for about two hours, kept a steady up pace of learning and planned ahead for the next lesson. I was paid in "wan" currency, at the equivalent of $10.00 per week. This was "big money" for me in 1956 on a G.I. payroll and the experience again, was great. It helped me set my goals for my civilian teaching once I left the military. I'm happy to report that the Korean officers did reach their goals and could carry on a well structured conversation in

English when our series of lessons were finished. We had a wonderful picnic together (with their families) in a local park and spoke only English. It was very pleasant.

Another experience I had while I was stationed in Korea was to tutor a young lady in English and American History at our base library for several weeks. These were tutoring sessions and we made excellent progress in her achieving her goals of passing various tests. Passing these tests were very important for it helped her to secure a position at her job.

When I fulfilled my military service I was honorably discharged and returned stateside to Rochester, NY. I started a position with the Rochester City School District in 1957 and pursued my Master's Degree in Educational Administration and later some post graduate work at the U. of R. before moving on to the administrative field. My first teaching position was that of a 6th and 7th grade teacher at Schools No. 21 and No. 40 in the Rochester City School District. All of my goals for the future started in my numerous positions in the RCSD. I felt that each position would give me more background of the principles toward moving up the ladder in education.... as I had a desire or feeling of accomplishing the next chapter of my career.

Sometimes a person can have a desire but not have the mental attitude to move on so I had to keep that in my mind all the time. I looked at each day as a total for casting of tomorrow but also letting each tomorrow take care of itself with proper preparation and experience to move on. I always felt that the foundation we build each day of our career has to be solid and bring joy in our work, especially working with children. If that is not felt in your present position, then it may be necessary to change directions and modify those principles for another role in your career.

I was asked to become a Co-Director of ABC's Project Headstart in the City of Rochester. Together with a co-director, Sister Joanne, R.S.M., we managed a team of 22 teachers and other educational personnel in reaching out to over 100 children at 17 different locations around the City of Rochester. This was a seven week program for needy inner-city youngsters entering kindergarten. This was a very rewarding experience for all of us.

As stated earlier, I became a helping teacher (vice principal) in the mid 1960's and a year later a principal. (See Appendix II for a list of the schools where I served as principal). I first retired in 1990 after twenty-five years as a principal. I then instituted the first substitute principal position in RCSD and subbed for 10 years. I really enjoyed this new position and facet of my career. Many of my colleagues from administration joined me in this new endeavor. I re-retired in 2000 and on numerous occasions I worked with students at Schools 2 and 42 in my son Alex's classroom. I tutored the students as well as teaching them some basic Korean, Polish or making a homemade pizza from scratch (steps in a procedure). My tutoring at other schools also included helping children in reading and junior high math.

I wanted to mention the above as a total of my educational involvement to give the "big picture" of all the principles I gathered along my educational path of my work as a teacher and principal for 33 years and 10 additional years as a substitute principal for a total of some 45 years (including teaching during my military service). In this reflection, I worked diligently to do the best work I could in each so that the next step would be a welcomed effort in moving on. No, not change for change's sake but rather a feeling of another "mountain to climb" and finding different ways to help students reach their life's goal of a good education.

In the following chapters, I will try to focus on meaning of each role in building a career for myself and having a good profession for my family and myself so as to support our five sons and helping them gain the educational roles from pre-school education (of course mom being their first teacher in many ways in the early years), elementary and secondary education, college work and grad college work in fields of education, law, finance and related areas.

As I reflect now in my retirement years of the various achievements in education, I cannot help but think of my other principles of career planning in my early years of life. Serious considerations were to go into medicine (being a medical doctor), law enforcement with the FBI or State Police. I feel now that I could have been successful in these other careers but the circumstances were such that the field of education was the brightest light in my career focus. I believe I made a wise decision since I have enjoyed working in the field with children, other teachers and parents throughout the years. I also felt that as a certified teacher, I could also assist better in teaching our sons the fundamentals of a good education. Apparently it worked well for me since all five of our sons did graduate from colleges and graduate schools as well.

Life itself is an education. Be it a formal diploma or an informal education in skill work; all leads to building those principles of where do you want to be in life as the years quickly move on for each of us. I always felt that each day brings on new knowledge and we learn each day. Life is a school of learning, building, helping others to learn and finally putting all to work for you and for society. Seeking those goals became a routine for me as I moved from one position to another in my career. Even during the years in my military career, the thought went through my mind if I should remain in the Army and build a career as an officer since that would be possible with a college degree in my hand and moving on to a higher rank as some of my friends did in those years. I decided that the military life was not in my future so I went back into civilian life pursuing a career as a school teacher and administrator.

As I conclude this chapter of my own background in my educational career, I want the reader to understand that each step in my career was from conversations with family, friends and reading up on different goals in the field of education. This step by step planning was sometimes by design (with some deep thinking at times) and other times by being at the right place at the right time for a move forward. I am pleased that I took the time to review possible steps in my career and listen to others who gave me insightful advice as I made the decisions to move ahead.

CHAPTER 6

Creating the New Role of the Substitute Principal
in the Rochester City School District

I would like to touch upon the many different things I have done to make the field of education more productive and efficient for many teachers, children, parents and the RCSD. In order to do this, one has to be creative and always be aware of what is ahead and how to get there for the good of the system. By system, of course I am referring to basically way we educate the children since they are the reason we are in this business. One statement I like in this regard is: "There can be different problems in life but these can become the many opportunities to achieve and therefore solve them". This can be done with careful team efforts and consultation between this team of teachers, parents, central office personnel and even children. Often times, one idea can spark another idea in the team and forward motion is made and success can be seen beyond the next "mountain".

One of the things I wanted to focus on was what happens when the principal has to be out of the school building for few hours to perhaps many weeks? How do you cover the school leadership, discipline needs, school supply needs, contacts with parents, etc.? How can the needs be met of parent / principal conferences, meetings and even illness happens when the principal is not there!

Whenever I and the many other principals were not able to be in the building, it would be necessary to ask a reliable classroom teacher to be "teacher in charge" as the acting principal (unless you had a vice principal which many schools did not have). I had done this for many years from my first year as principal until the last years leading up to my first retirement. When I was about to retire, I thought that there must be a better way to cover the school's office when leadership was absent. Again, as I said earlier, one has to focus on what is ahead and how to get there for the good of the system. I thought that if we cover the important position of a classroom substitutes, why not cover the same with a substitute principal and one of my principles of good action for the sake of the school. Another reason I had for this kind of replacement was that whenever I asked a teacher to be "teacher in charge" for my position, I would have to hire a substitute teacher for this teacher and disturb the classroom routine with a sub that may or may not do a good a job as the regular teacher. Therefore, all the more reason to get a good sub to cover my position as principal when I was away from my office.

When I was retired just a few weeks, I received a call from one of my friends who was still active as the principal and she asked me if I could cover for her for the day while she was attending a meeting of school principals. I said, "for sure, since that is what I was thinking of doing when I retired...at least for a year of so". Now she told me in order to do so, I needed to call Human Services at our Personnel Office and get a "PIN "number for payroll purposes. I did call Central Office and the head of personnel said, "Are you substituting as a teachers?" I said, "No, as the principal of the school". The reply was, "we have no such category for the job". Well my reply was, "then let us start the category and I can cover the principal's position for the day at the teacher's sub rate since there was no budget to cover for a principal". "Fine, we can do that" said the head of Human Resources....and we did. I became the FIRST substitute principal in the Rochester City School District and went on to do this work for the next ten years. This is another example of how in a career, you can consider a particular of need and help formulate a plan of action for the improvement of the schools for the sake of the children.

I thought I would sub for a year or two but went on with my substitute work for the next 10 years and enjoyed it very much. I had a lot of satisfaction in this new position since it gave me a "fading away" role from what I did for the past 27 years. It gave my retirement years the feeling of being away from a full time position but still involved in the routine of being the principal....even for a day or two. The fading into my new role gave me an opportunity to see many different schools in the district in their differing styles of operation. It also gave me a chance to visit my son Alex at Clara Barton School No. 2 where he taught for 21 years. I so enjoyed going to his school that I started to do most of my substitute assignments at School No. 2 rather than hopping around to different schools. While I was working in this new role, a number of other retired principals heard of my work and started to join "our new team" of retired personnel in administration. I did advise some of my fellow retirees of the steps involved in becoming a substitute principal and many started to return to the schools in the months and years that followed.

When I went to a number of schools to substitute, I not only helped keep the school in balance while the regular principal was away but learned some new techniques that were present and could share that with other school personnel. This was interesting and enjoyable as part of my role. The salary of only getting a small stipend for my sub work rather than the larger income that the principal would earn did not bother me since I did have a retirement income from the New York State Retirement System and in a few years later my social security income came in. Actually I did this work not to earn extra income but to assure that the schools were properly covered and again doing something inventive in the field of education, in the Rochester City School District.

At times, this new role was a challenge when I met children and parents that did not know me but after a number of days and sometimes weeks as I returned to some of these same schools, I got to know the staff, children and parents as well and felt a feeling of closeness with them all. This was the greatest gift of doing this work, the feeling of doing something worthwhile in my early years of retirement as I also looked forward to different activities of retirement years.

I would like to share some of my activities in retirement years with the reader at this point. This information will give the reader a better understanding of not only what I have and am doing in the past administrative field of endeavor but will give a deeper understanding of "moving on" in life after any job or professional work. This is most necessary in order to have a zest of life in "doing for others" even in retirement as one does in the work years.

I continued to be involved in church groups, American Legion, professional associations as well as social groups in order to learn more, assist people and enjoy the involvement. The church groups were always there but now I could be more deeply involved with each of these groups and associations. Also became more involved with the American Legion Post 134 located in Irondequoit as the Vice Commander and Public Relations Officer. Also the RTO (Retired Teachers/ Educators Organization) became a big part of my retirement life. This continued to give a good contact with educators as well as a personal involvement with old and new friends.

The point I am trying to make here is that anytime in life and in any kind of professional or regular work in life, one needs to "look forward" in making your mark in life for others to follow and have the good feeling of accomplishment in life. Often I heard about people being bored in life after retirement or being sorry that they did retire and did not "die with their boots on" in their work. I feel that as each stage of life enters the picture of "your life", you need to accept it all and move forward with new thoughts which become new ideas that become new accomplishments…be they small or gigantic, never-the-less, the next stage of your life to give and enjoy anew.

As I move on in my thinking of ideas and achievements after work years, I feel that looking back on those many years of my principles at work give me a feeling of joy, satisfaction, pride and even a little wonderment of "how did I do it all" in those years now past. I believe the answer may be that we all take one day at a time and that becomes the total of years and a career to look back on for one to enjoy and share with others as I am trying to do with my writing this book for you, the reader.

CHAPTER 7

A Look Ahead in Education…as a Retired Principal…

…for Principles Ahead

Where have we been and where are we going? This is probably the most important part of my book. The review of my career may speak for itself, but the important question is now, "where"? Where are we going?

I am sure that every educator on earth may have ideas for the future as we move along our path of life in the field of our challenges and outcomes. Most likely they are all important if…I say again, IF the student is in the center of our goal. True, the challenges involve financial needs to run a school, from a small one room schoolhouse in the depths of Africa or South American to the large ivy covered Universities throughout the world. And there may be problems of securing staff, material, equipment, funds etc. in order to run the schools. But the very strong focus has to be on the student…to engage him/her in a meaningful challenge, motivate the desire to explore, build a love of learning and build a team to reach these steps along the way. These mentioned material needs are important but with willing givers and a strong principle to build a good nation and a network of nations, it will take a team of people to do it. This team is comprised of you and

I....the basic true believer of reaching every student in building the desire to learn...learn and learn more.

I would like to move in the direction of projecting my outcomes in the various principles already sited into the future and dreaming a little more about where we can and perhaps should be in the years ahead.

As we look at the student (child, young adult, adult), we as educators must see beyond this individual and see the "finished product" of our efforts in the years or work. The lessons at the first years of the education, the lectures, field trips, many book reviews, maps, discoveries, writings, discussions, etc. all center on the student reaching the ultimate goal of learning. The maximum of what the student wants to achieve. This site must be seen in our mind as we start the progress. All of this is necessary if we are to reach the end successfully. All too often, we as teachers, administrators, look at what is happening today and worry about the problems of today or tomorrow but fail to look at where we would like to see the students in years ahead and yes, where the student himself/herself would like to be in the goal setting of their life's career. As educators, we must have a sight beyond today and keep that goal constantly in our mind for the sake of the student and successfully reaching our goals as educators...be we teachers or school administrators and certainly parents too.

Let me paint a picture for you from my many years of working with students, parents, educators and various people who want the best for their child and for America.

Success...yes, success in accomplishing a good career and a good life of reaching out to people and building for the next generation to come. This can be done in many ways of course but I feel the most important way is to be personally involved in the goal setting and working every step along the way to reach these accomplishments.

The picture that I wish to paint here is a student entering school for the first time...naive and inexperienced and looking for good guidance from the educators. The students wants a clear understanding of what can and must be done in order to learn, enjoy and involve all aspects of learning. These can involve the books, the many media of learning that are presented and receive good guidance to reach many goals whether learning the ABCs or training to be a successful doctor or lawyer at the university. What I am trying to paint here is my projection of the educator in the principles of good teaching and learning day by day...all the time keeping "an eye" on the successful goal in the years ahead.

I can see schools of tomorrow being developed in working with accomplished successful leaders and professionals who can devote time to have the learner work together...not like now for a short span of time but for years being in contact with each other between the classroom and the work area....with the professional educator keeping a clear record of what is happening and what happens next to reach success in time.

The "open door classroom" is now happening here and there as it has for years. But the question is, "what principles are being held by the educators to track and motivate students"? These principles as I have been writing about in the preceding pages are all aimed toward having a strong and clear picture on the student to accomplish each and every experience along the path of learning. As a principal, I made this my measure with teachers and parents to constantly evaluate the student and move along this path in every way possible to be successful and not thinking of becoming a "drop out" or lacking an interest in learning since "no one cares"....so "why should I care". This should never be in the learners mind…or at least not for very long since good motivation must be coming forth from the family, school and even the community.

This is a brief picture that I paint for the child of the future…a very productive, motivated, and concerned student that wants to learn because all care and there is a real good reason why we all need each other to be successful in life.

I always felt that as an educator (teacher, principal) I wanted to set good goals and role models for children to want to learn and every support we can develop must be ready to administer for the sake of the student moving along the path of the learning road.

I feel I have done that and still do with people I meet today, in an out of school experience. The world is our stage and we are the motivated individuals that will make things work successfully if we keep an eye on the future and keep in focus. We all need each other and support is part of our life.

As part of this painting of the child entering school, the friendly atmosphere needs to be established and held constantly for the young learner. Being relaxed in a pleasant atmosphere will be the foundation of the child to "want" to learn and of course enjoy school. This needs to be a part of every classroom from Kindergarten to the High School level and beyond as well. Being comfortable in a situation makes learning stronger and more enjoyable. In my years of work in the field of education, I found at times not a warm, friendly atmosphere and therefore the lack of learning desire on the part of the learner. This in my estimation is a must and much learning will follow.

Parents are always an important part of the team to learn and must be in constant communication with the school. The team is not complete unless the "foundation of this child from home" is not present and part of the action. If a parent reading this book finds a situation of not being involved, I strongly urge that parent to step forth and make it know that he/she wants and needs to be part of the educational team. This I believe improves chances of success over 100% when a sincere and interested parent steps up to the plate and lend a hand often to build upon the future of the child in reaching each goal along the line of education. This is true at the very beginning until college and even graduate school to encourage and motivate the learner to move ahead. The future depends on all of us to do our part…in some small way or at a major way for building success…that word again, "success" since we all want to see it happen for all our learners.

Once the team approach is complete and moving on, I can suggest "hands on learning" as was mentioned earlier so that the real world of work and occupation will be apparent to the learner. This future projection will allow all kinds of learning media to be available with the micro-chip and internet systems allowing much faster learning to actually "being there" at the scene of learning. This scene can be the workplace, the court, the hospital, the office, the church, the operating room, the radio/TV station, the flight control system and on and on. All this will be available soon to the learner and that is good. Great strides will make all this possible if we work as a team to build success for the learner from the very start of teaching a pre-school learner the foundation for school and learning and up to higher education. I wish at times that I, in my later part of life, could start again to work with learners, especially all that I have learned in life as an educator and parent and grandparent. This is why I was motivated to put into print my ideas from years of learning so that the parent, teacher, Principal could have a solid foundation to start new and reach up to (here is that word again) success for every child and learner that desires to learn about the world around him/her. I know it can be done!

All learners are just waiting for role models and we can be that for them, especially children who need a goal to reach for each day. Every parent, single individual, educator (at all levels) can shine for the learner if we take the time to do so. Our expectations are to "show the way" to success …even with some trials along the road to the goals...."go for it".

CHAPTER 8

Some Thoughts to Consider in Doing the World's Most Important Work... Teaching Children and Others to Aspire to a Greater Life

As I think back to the start of my career as a teacher, aspiring to go into school administration, I had this in mind... what do I want to do in education? I wanted to react to the needs of the school system as a parent, advisor to other teachers, and a community participant. I believe I reached that goal in different ways and today, even in retirement, I still want to be a part of the educational society in helping where I can. In retirement I became active with helping high school students with college funds by being active in the American Legion's Scholarship Committee, and as a member of the Scholarship Committee of the Polish Heritage Society of Rochester.

As the reader looks at a career in education, you have to have a wide view of our society and the needs for building success for our nation through the school systems...starting with the first "school", the family. As we advance ourselves into the folds of a career in education, learning a wide variety of subjects, the need is always there to reach out to people in a positive way and build, build and go on building for the future.

Now you are ready to advance yourself into a career of teaching and possibly go on to an administrative position. You need to stay on course in good studies and build a well-rounded education. Your practice or internship in schools builds your interest and gives you the experience in working with children, parents, your supervisors and the community. This all goes into the "bank of knowledge" as you move ahead in the field of your study. All along the way, you have good knowledge of positive roles you want to have in mind so that when the big day comes to take on your first class or your first position as a school principal, your principles will be in the right order to start from day one and on to a good career in education. This in a brief way is the route to travel on as you move from year to year onto success for the student and society. Positive thoughts with building your energy into one success after another and letting any errors turn into accomplishments with corrections as needed.

All along your path to positive accomplishments, keep the student as the main focus ….reaching out in all ways to make learning pleasurable, interesting, positive and successful. Each day is a journey to the successful outcome. If problems develop, turn them into success the next day with some correction and help from the team of teachers, parents and your own desire to succeed.

One day at a time....success is at the end of your rainbow. This is the best advice I can share at this point of reviewing my career in education. The world of education is the foundation of our society and you are then a big part of it as your walk through life.

CHAPTER 9

A Reflection on Good Administration
Alex J. Johnson, National Board Certified Teacher, 2011

I am very proud to have had my father serve so many students and teachers as a principal over a 35 year time period. I know that from the number of colleagues that I have worked with that had also worked with my Dad that he was a fair and approachable administrator.

In my thirty-one years of teaching in both the Catholic and public schools of Rochester, NY I have worked for ten principals and eleven vice principals. As you can imagine, I have seen a wide range of management styles of the administrators as they worked with other administrators, parents, students and the teaching staff. The principal really sets the tone of the building be it good, bad or indifferent. They are the leader of the building, should be a master teacher and set an example for the teaching staff and the students. Most lead by example and really try to foster a fair sense family and community within their schoolhouse.

The principals that I have really enjoyed working for have given me a sense of being a part of a team to not only increase student performance but to become more involved in building school spirit. This encouragement pushes many teachers to work beyond the contractual school day and to go into "extra innings" for their school. This may be in the form of taking additional professional development workshops, tutoring students / after school, becoming involved in many school or district-wide committees or just spending additional hours working in their own classrooms after the students are dismissed. As I said, I feel motivated to do such when I feel that I am valued member of the school's team. Camaraderie between teachers is usually very strong and working collaboratively is very important for the strength of the grade levels and working vertically up and down through the grade levels with other teachers. It is always a major plus when the camaraderie can extend to the administrators as well. Teachers and other staff need to know that they are valued by the administration for them to work as diligently as they do.

I have had had some administrators who have valued the time and effort that I have put into classroom, school and district-wide programs. Some have put letters of praise into my personnel file and others have taken the kudos and recognition that I have received and used it to their advantage with their own direct supervisors. I don't mind it when they happen to use my kudos to help themselves, as I do work for them, but I don't think it's fair when the same administrators then blame you for failures and take none on themselves. Unfortunately some educators go into administration for the wrong reasons.

I personally feel that a quality administrator needs at least ten years in a classroom to really get the true feel of teaching. Ideally a classroom background in general education and special education would best serve the candidates' toolbox of education knowledge before they become an administrator. I feel that a great administrator really has a well-rounded background and strives to inspire their faculty and students. As stated before, they lead by example and will easily model for their teachers examples of masterful teaching. Many of my twenty-one administrators have fit into this mode. They are the ones that I am thankful for and have encouraged me. Their job has long hours, dozens of meetings with Central Office, teachers, parents, community groups, school committees, etc. The effective administrators make their schools work well and create a real positive environment conducive to learning. A caring family atmosphere is noticeable and the staff, students and visitors are made to feel accepted and welcome. Again the attitude of the administrator can make or break a building's spirit. Schools that are shepherded by such a principal are the ones where test scores rise, have strong school spirit, aren't put on a "closing list" and often have a waiting list of teachers and students that want to be a part of that school.

I was always impressed and inspired when I would visit my Dad's schools. I began working for the RCSD "off the books" by stamping incoming textbooks at School No. 30 every August in the late 1960's. My brothers and I would often go to school with Dad when our school in West Irondequoit had off. My first substitute teaching gig was when my Dad asked me to sub for Mrs. Riley at School No. 25 back in the Spring of 1982. When I visited my Dad's schools, the teachers and students often didn't know who I was and would speak candidly about how great their school was. I witnessed my Dad at several faculty breakfasts cooking and serving food in the faculty lounge. I saw him deliver great, inspiring messages at evening performances. As recently as November 2011 he was invited back to School No. 36 where he had been principal to take part in their annual Veterans' Day Recognition program. It made me feel proud when my college classmate Paul, now the principal of the building, recognized my Dad for his years with the district and past leadership of his building. Kudos to my Dad!

CHAPTER 10

Personal Thanks to my Family, the R.C.S.D., Local Colleges, and the Thousands of Parents and Students

A big smile and thanks for all those who helped to make it all possible...starting out with my good principles developed throughout my life from childhood for a good school system. These principles were to work for the child (student of any age) in being a motivator for good learning and being a good role model for study, getting along with people and building the desire to learn.

I would like to thank the many people in my life that I have worked with in the many years (45 yrs.) in my professional life in the field of education.

Thanks to the universities as the State University of New York at Brockport, University of Rochester and John Fisher College, Military Language training, etc. with their helpful professors that gave me the background and forward knowledge to develop my skills in education.

The early start at the age of 17 of going to SUNY Brockport, built a solid foundation in my setting of goals of where I wanted to go in time. Year by year, the thoughts of becoming a doctor or teacher ran through my mind as I grew in knowledge and understanding of what is ahead for me in life. As the university years moved on, my thoughts went to educating people who may become nurses, doctors, lawyers, engineers, truck drivers, machinists, etc. became apparent. So, as an educator, I wanted to strive toward and maybe move into the career as a school administrator (principal). The principle role of becoming a principal became seated in my mind. The wonderful parents that I worked with…who showed care and love for their children – I thank them in helping me to meet the anticipated expectations in my work. Some parents were a challenge at times but my principles of my work became their principles too.

As I worked with many students who were not sure of which career to choose, I tried to give some insight to them about where they would like to go in their planning. An interest in a specialized field is the first step in making a choice. Then the ability to learn the skills needed to enter the field is next since much learning has to be gained in the years ahead before mastery is accomplished for the work to be done. Then a projection of one's self into the years ahead is valuable in order to visualize what can lie ahead....are you ready to do this work day after day and year after year. Are you ready to take on the changes that may be necessary in order to accomplish your goals and satisfy your superiors in order to complete the work successfully? All this must be held in the learners mind in order to proceed ahead.

I tried to have this in my mind as I looked forward to my career and attempted to show this role to others who were "thinking of doing the job" in their future. Of course there are some that desire to change their career or need to do so ….this will involve another similar review of "can I do this and do I have the ability to reach my goal" in this new endeavor or chapter of my life. All this has to be kept in mind as we look forward to success in a career in a life of work.

For my being able to accomplish what I had a desire to do in my formative early life, I thank all who had a part in my path on the road to success…I thank you all.

The principles that I learned early in life from parents, teachers, professors and others in education, led me to that role of being a principal to help others in their learning and accomplishments through the years of my work and now beyond in my retirement years still working with people...i.e. volunteer work, assisting different organizations and friends in "working it out" for a good feeling about their own life.

After 45 years as an educator, I felt it was time to "move on" to retirement life as a volunteer in education and other organizations that function for the benefit of children and others in our society.

It is good for an individual to involve once self into society to help others "see the outcome of a good education" and help project people in a focus of what they are doing and what they can do. It is amazing what we can do if we allow ourselves to look forward...regardless of your age. Young, older or much older, everyone can get involved in helping others to contribute more principles to a good life and meaningful one too.

For a brief review of my volunteer work, I would like to point out some of my involvement in the community.

I am a Vice Commander with the American Legion Post and volunteer to be a part of this great organization that helps other veterans and people in need in the community. As an example, we go to the Veterans Hospital in Canandaigua in the summer and at Christmas time to give Veterans a nice time and cheer them up since they gave so much to their country. I also volunteer as a "Service Officer" to send cheering cards to sick members and direct a "last farewell" to deceased members of our Post,

I also help out on occasion at my son Alex's school by volunteering in his classroom when time allows. It certainly brings back memories of my work as a teacher and an administrator in the school system.

We also volunteer to assist in a senior adult club at one of our community parishes in helping members to enjoy a social involvement with each other. Also other parish work as time allows to impart the principles of positive action to help others.

All of these activities (only mentioning a few) give me a good feeling of giving back to the community some of the principles and skills of being a principal for years and now giving outside of the school environment.

I trust others, like yourself, will step up and do something constructive for our society to help others as we did with children in years past and now in our community and the years beyond.

CHAPTER 11

Final Thoughts for Those That Aspire to the Field of Education as either Teachers or Administrators

Many books have been written on the subject on taking the first steps into the field of education and I would like to share a few pointed values for the reader to think about and perhaps act upon in the year or years ahead.

I believe, as I look back in my many years in education, that a solid commitment must be made to dedicate oneself to help the children (learners) to help them reach a strong goal in getting a quality education. Also, a school leader (principal) should have a varied background in a good understanding of the learning process in order to guide other teachers to a successful outcome. I have felt that with my many different roles in education beyond the classroom, I had the ability to help set goals for teachers and children and show them the many varied roads to reach their individual goals.

In years to come, the goals may remain the same as they are today…i.e. exploring the many avenues of a career and developing a positive attitude toward study and learning but they may be developed in different ways. The available technologies such as the PC and Mac computers, iPods, iPads, iPhones, Droids, Kindles, Nooks and social media such as Facebook and Twitter will have a very active role in education as the curriculum is written for them for instruction. Even joining Facebook and getting ideas from others "on line" in their careers may help motivate a person to go forward. I would also project that people who are successful in their careers will be more inclined to work together with schools to share their skills and achievements as role models for others to follow. This I feel very important since success breeds more success for others to follow. There are so many successful doctors, lawyers, engineers, business people, nurses, etc. that can help show the way to the learner of the way to go on in reaching that career. I trust that people who read this information will have a kindly reminder to do so…even if not asked to do so, but to volunteer to a learning institution to be active in this regard. That is my hope….

Schools of the future may not look like the institutions of learning that we know today. They may be more "on the job training" areas where electronic gear may bring the learner closer to the actual learning of the skill or technique of their chosen career. Of course, it will always be necessary to have a broad foundation for the career to come. This will have to be guided by solid instructors or teachers who have a concrete understanding of the possible or desired outcome for the leaner. These instructors or teachers will have to be given good guidance from the leaders (principal, headmasters, supervisors, deans, etc.) who can engage the clear principles of learning as the aforementioned guidance that is necessary.

As we look into the future, I would like to quote a statement that sound very solid to me for moving forward: "The only thing standing between ME and greatness is ME. Certainly I think a thought to keep in mind as we strive toward individual and collective achievements in life.

I believe we all should identify a goal to reach for in life. Be it a career, position of achievement or an opportunity to do something worthwhile in the person's mind. This goal should be realistic and something that the individual would enjoy doing in life. This can start for a very young person or even for a retired person who has completed one career already. Every day is a new start and a beginning for the future…be it a long future or a shorter one since no one knows the time. I felt this way in my younger years starting out for college from my high school in Niagara Falls and even in my retirement years after spending over 43 years with the

Rochester City School District. Always reach for a goal....that is what makes life interesting and productive. -A thought for you to ponder.

I have taken these last few months in collecting my thoughts of the past many years in education and work in other related areas. As all these thoughts came to mind, I felt I needed to record these many recollections so that as the years fade on, I will be able to recall the active years of my life in working with children and other learners. Also, I wanted to share my working career with our many family members, many of them who have gone into education, or who may be interested in understanding what they can do in life.

I wrote this book, as I did my autobiography in 2009, in order to record for the present and future readers our family's history and culture. Copies of my autobiography can be found in the Monroe County public libraries as well as our family members' homes and at the SUNY College at Brockport for friends and others to enjoy and perhaps learn from my career experiences.

APPENDIX I: MY EDUCATIONAL TIMELINE

A Chronological Timeline on How I Reached My Professional Goals

In a follow-up of my thanks to so many, I would like to share a timeline of my years leading up to and continuing in the field of education.

1950 - Graduated from Niagara Falls High School in Niagara Falls, NY

1950 - Entered into my first year at the State University of New York at Brockport as an education major in elementary education,

1954 - Graduated from SUNY Brockport with a B.S. degree in education for teaching elementary school.

1955 - Entered the U.S. Army from the Army Reserve which I was a member
for several years prior to full time military service.

1955 - Trained at Personnel Management School at Ft. Harrison, Indiana with a specialty in Military Record Keeping.

-Taught Elementary School in Indianapolis, Indiana awaiting orders to be assigned overseas for military duty in Korea.

1956 -Assigned to SMP (Seoul Military Post) 8th Army HQ in Seoul, Korea....work on Officers 201 files in office duty.
-Taught Korean officers English at a Korean Military Engineer School near Seoul, Korea (12 adult military students).

- Discharged myself from the Army at Ft. Dix, N.J. due to my past experience in personnel work.

-Fall late admission at SUNY Brockport for Master's degree in Administrative Education.

1957 -Started my teaching position with the City School District as an elementary school teacher at School No. 21 for three years.

1958 -Earned my M.S. degree in Administration from SUNY in the spring as I continued teaching at the elementary school.

1961 -Advanced to "Helping Teacher" with the RCSD after teaching five years in the Classroom. Worked at 10 schools with probationary teachers moving toward their tenure goal.

1962 -Achieved position as vice principal in three schools during this year. Two schools in one semester and one in the other semester.

1963 -Advanced to principal at Monroe School No. 15.

1967 -Summer....became the first co-director of Project Headstart under a federal grant with ABC Early Childhood Education. Worked with
Sister Mary Joann and a staff of many teachers, aides, speech personnel, and social workers.

1968 -Upgraded to larger schools in the next few years. **Schools No. 30, No. 36, No. 25, and No. 50** (many of which included vice-principals and more staff to assist running the school). I was co-principal with John Thomas at **No. 19** but moved the second semester to **No. 5** following the death of Peter Castle. The following year I started at **No. 50**.

1990 -Retired from the RCSD and moved on....

1991 -Became the first substitute principal in the RCSD and continued in this
position until 2000 when I re-retired to do volunteer work and stay active with numerous organizations.

In my movement through the various of positions and different schools in the Rochester City School District, I met thousands of people who assisted me in reaching these positions. I would like to thank all of them again… now in writing. Their guidance, inspiration, encouragement, goal setting, and kind words all helped me reach my goals and to be able to help others throughout the years. Now, in retirement, I still feel I can help others in my volunteer work as I venture on in my work to "help others".

APPENDIX II: SCHOOLS WHERE I SERVED

School No. 41 (Kodak Park School)   279 W. Ridge Rd.

School No. 15 (Monroe School)   494 Averill Ave.

School No. 30 (General Elwell S. Otis School)   36 Otis St.

School No. 36 (Henry W. Longfellow School)   85 St. Jacob St.

School No. 25 (Nathaniel Hawthorne School)   965 N. Goodman St.

School No. 19 (Dr. Charles T. Lunsford School)   465 Seward St.

School No. 5 (John Williams School)   555 N. Plymouth Ave.

School No. 50 (Helen Barrett Montgomery School) 507 Seneca Ave.

APPENDIX III: DOCUMENTS

SUNY Brockport Graduate School Acceptance Letter   1957

SUNY Brockport Master's Exam Pass / Fail Letter	1957
NYS Administration Degree Probationary Certificate	1962
Headstart Program newspaper article	1965
RCSD Superintendent Herman Goldberg Letter	1965
Cathleen Corbet Letter to Dr. Young	1978
RCSD Acting Superintendent H. Hunter Fraser Strike Letter	1980
A.S.A.R. Article about Substitute Principals in RCSD	1991

STATE UNIVERSITY OF NEW YORK
TEACHERS COLLEGE AT BROCKPORT
BROCKPORT, NEW YORK

January 24, 1957

Mr. Alexander C. Johnson
16 Pulzski Street
Rochester 21, New York

Dear Mr. Johnson:

Your request for matriculation in the graduate program leading to the Master of Science degree at the State University Teachers College at Brockport has been acted upon favorably by the Graduate Council.

Sincerely,

George Anselm
Director of Graduate Studies

GA:BP

Results of the Master's Written

Comprehensive Examination in Education

NAME OF CANDIDATE *Alexander Johnson*

Passed: ✓   Failed: _____

Date *July 27, 1957*   Signed ....
George Anselm
Director of Teacher Education

The University of the State of New York
The State Education Department

PROVISIONAL CERTIFICATE

Be it known that ALEXANDER CHESTER JOHNSON having satisfied the minimum requirements prescribed by the State Education Department is hereby granted this certificate, valid for the period described on the reverse for service as a Principal (elementary) in the public schools.

In witness whereof, *the Education Department under its seal at Albany, New York, grants this Certificate No. 62EP12722 effective September 1, 1962*

Commissioner of Education

Chief, Bureau of Teacher Education and Certification

READYING "HEAD START" PROGRAM, due to begin on July 6, are (from left) Miss Alice Ferrari and Mrs. Alice Young, Supervisors, Alexander Johnson and Sister M. Joanne, co-Directors and Frank Rinere, Social Worker. Visual aids were a topic at this planning session.

Head Start Plan Ready to Roll

Some 660 inner-city youngsters who will be entering school this fall are due to get a helpful "Head Start" from the project of the same name starting in 17 centers on July 6.

Co-directors of "Operation Head Start" in Rochester are two grammar school principals, Alexander Johnson of School 15 on Averill Avenue and Sister M. Joanne, R.S.M., of St. Thomas the Apostle School in Irondequoit.

The centers will be staffed by about 22 professional teachers, and approximately the same number of teacher aides drawn from the neighborhoods around each center.

Several Catholic institutions are among the 17 locations for the nursery school-type centers. They are:

Mt. Carmel Church, St. Bridget's Church, Immaculate Conception Church, St. Lucy's Church, Holy Redeemer Church, SS. Peter and Paul's Church and St. Francis Xavier.

A 2-day orientation program for teachers and aides was scheduled for Catherine McAuley College this week.

Sister Joanne said that the directors are looking for some volunteers, high school or college students, who could escort some of the youngsters to and from the Head Start locations, and help at each center. Interested volunteers may contact Sister Joanne by calling FI 2-3311.

The Head Start operation comes under the federal anti-poverty program, which is administered locally by the Action for a Better Community (ABC) office.

The 7-week program for disadvantaged youngsters entering kindergarten, or if not in school last year, entering first grade, is a summer project only.

June 1965

CITY SCHOOL DISTRICT
13 Fitzhugh Street South
ROCHESTER, NEW YORK 14614
LOcust 2-3200

Herman R. Goldberg
Superintendent of Schools

August 20, 1965

Mr. Alexander Johnson
227 Belcoda Drive
Rochester, New York 14617

Dear Alex:

    Thank you very much for following through on the details for the presentation of Operation Headstart at the Board meeting yesterday. The very complete and careful way in which you took care of everything is greatly appreciated.

    Have a good vacation, short as it has to be.

Sincerely yours,

Herman R. Goldberg

HRG:ks

85 St. Jacob Street
Rochester, New York
School No. 36

Dr. Alice Young
13 S. Fitzhugh Street
Rochester, New York

Dear Dr. Young,

It is so seldom that any of us take the time to inform you personally whom we feel that someone is doing an admirable job in his position, yet we are usually quick to criticize.

Since I have been one of those quick to criticize, I would like to take this opportunity to offer praise for one of your employees, Mr. Alex Johnson, Principal of #36. During the school year 77-78, he has done a commendable job in our school. He has provided constant support to his teaching staff in many obvious ways. He has helped us greatly with discipline, with parents, and in numerous other ways. His "open door policy" makes it possible for us to go to him at any time, without fear, to discuss any problem or concern we may have.

It has been a pleasure to work with him this year as a member of his staff.

Sincerely,
Cathleen M. Corbet, Teacher

January 3, 1978

CITY SCHOOL DISTRICT
131 WEST BROAD STREET
ROCHESTER, NEW YORK 14608
716-325-4560

RECEIVED
School No. 25
Date 9/15/80

H. HUNTER FRASER
Acting Superintendent of Schools

September 10, 1980

Mr. Alexander Johnson
Principal
School No. 25
965 Goodman Street North
Rochester, New York 14609

Dear Mr. Johnson: *Alex,*

    During this period of great personal and professional stress, I want you to know how deeply I appreciate your support. Your responsibilities have multiplied along with your pressures. You have undergone threats, harassments, and vandalism and have even faced physical danger in order to try to help the City School District carry out its responsibilities to students, parents, and the community.

    You have done all this knowing that at some point the strike will be settled and that it will be your responsibility to work with staff who have been on the picket line, and to deal with the emotional aftereffects that will be felt by staff on both sides of the issue, as well as by students and parents.

    The job of a school principal is a difficult one in the best of times. During this trying period, you have earned even greater gratitude and respect from me, other members of the District's central management team and the Board of Education. Your contributions to this school district have not gone unnoticed.

    All of the efforts of the Board and the central administration are being devoted to getting the schools re-opened as soon as possible.

                                 Sincerely,

                                   H. HUNTER FRASER

cc: Ms. Genovese, President
    Members of the Board of Education

ADMINISTRATORS AND SUPERVISORS

Retired Administrators Still Working for School District

On July 15, 1991, Governor Cuomo signed into law legislation (Chapter 302 of the laws of 1991) which increases earnings allowed for retirees employment (public sector) from $9,360 to $9,720 and indications are that it will be a higher amount in the near future. All this has been done to encourage retirees to re-enter the public sector job market to assist school district in different ways.

The Board of Directors of S.A.A.N.Y.S. Region 11, has asked the Retired Principal Representatives on their Board and the Regional Field Representatives to look into the utilization of retired administrators as substitute personnel. The plan was started in March 1991 by Alexander Johnson substituting for Principal Norma Bushorr of School No. 25 in Rochester. Nine additional administrators have worked for the City School District. The idea is growing not only in the city but also in the suburban areas as well.

Our S.A.A.N.Y.S. regional Board of Directors has approved a substitute Administrative plan whereby requests from over 10 school districts are included in such a program. Districts will be able to select from a pool of substitute administrators as the need arises. This pool will be made up of retired school administrators that wish to use their years of experience in helping many newer administrators for short or long term assignments. The district negotiates with each individual as to a per diem amount for the work assignment.

At the time of this writing, the Region 11 Board of Directors is acting as facilitator in setting up the program in assisting District Superintendents in the Administrative Substitute plan.

APPENDIX IV: PHOTOGRAPHS

p. 89　ACJ in his former office at School No. 36

p. 90　Schools No. 15 and 30

p. 91　Schools No. 36 and 25

p. 92　School No. 50 and ACJ at that school

p. 93　ACJ in his 1950's US Army uniform
　　　　ACJ with "Madame Curie" at Sch. No. 42

p. 94　ACJ and Dan Johnson in Fulton, NY

p. 95　Alex Johnson Jr. with wife Laurie
　　　　ACJ and Ginny with Col. Pamela Melroy

p. 96　Virginia "Ginny" Gordinier Johnson

p. 97　My Life, My Dreams, My Hopes

Alex C. Johnson sitting at his old desk at School No. 36 with thoughts of the past….the principle role of the principal.

Monroe School No. 15
The first school that I was principal of in 1965.

Major General Elwell S. Otis School No. 30
I was principal at this building in the late 1960's

Longfellow School No. 36 is still the oldest building in the RCSD. I was here in the 1970's, parts of the building date back to 1896.

**Nathaniel Hawthorne School No. 25
I served here during the teacher's strike in 1980.**

Helen Montgomery School No. 50 This was the building that I retired from in 2000. It was also the closest school to our house in West Irondequoit.

Helen Montgomery School No. 50
Sitting in my last office with the RCSD.

Taken in 2012, this is the same uniform that I wore when I taught English to Korean Army officers in 1956.

Madame Curie (actress Susan Frontczak) at my son Alex's school in September 2011. She was a true role model as she spoke to grades 3 – 6 about her life as a scientist.

Visiting son Dan's school in Fulton, NY

**Dan Johnson when he served as principal at
James E. Lanigan Elementary School in Fulton, NY**

Ginny and ACJ with retired US Air Force Colonel Pam Melroy at School No. 42. Pam was one of the first female NASA astronauts to pilot and command a Space Shuttle.

ACJ's son Alex Johnson Jr. and his wife Laurie at a Rochester Teachers' Association meeting where Alex was recognized for achieving his National Board Teacher Certification. Alex is very proud of this prestigious accomplishment but more so of being able to help his father edit this book.

My wife Virginia "Ginny" Gordinier Johnson
who inspired and supported me along my career path in education.

My Life, My Dreams and My Hopes

The Autobiography of Alexander C. Johnson

If you enjoyed this book, you may also like to read ACJ's first book. Published by Lulu Books, the ISBN number for this edition is: 978-0-557-28815-1

Notes on your own "principles" as a principal...

Notes on your own "principles" as a principal...

Notes on your own "principles" as a principal...

Notes on your own "principles" as a principal...

Highlights from your own career...

Highlights from your own career...

Highlights from your own career...

Highlights from your own career...

A timeline of your career...

What is your most important "principle" that you would share with others?